CHILDREN OF THE NINETIES

PAT SIMMONS

redcliffe

First published in 1994 for
Children of the Nineties
University of Bristol by
Redcliffe Press Ltd, Bristol

ISBN 1 872971 93 8

British Library Cataloguing-in-Publication Data.
A catalogue record for this book is available
from the British Library.

*This book is dedicated to the parents and children
who are making it all possible*

Typeset and printed by The Longdunn Press Ltd., Bristol

Contents

ACKNOWLEDGEMENTS

I should like to thank the following: Caroline Brown for letting me quote her at such length; Joanna Webster-Green for giving up her time to talk to me; Jean Golding, Yasmin Iles-Caven, Pam Holmes and Sue Sadler for all their help; Maureen Brennan for taking most of the photos, and Hugh Simmons, without whose assistance I would never have got past Chapter 1.

Illustrations: Anne Fedrick.

Introduction

Little did I think when attending a meeting in Moscow in 1985 that I would be writing an introduction to a book that would be describing the exciting enterprise of mounting a study on over 14,000 parents and their children. The period in between has been exciting, frustrating and taxing, with various interesting features happening almost every day.

It was in order to explain to the many people taking part in this study how it happened that we asked Pat Simmons if she would like to write her own bird's eye view of the survey. She has documented here the way in which it started, who is involved, the trials and tribulations, the ups and downs of the whole study. This is a book that we hope will appeal not just to the people involved in the survey, but to everyone who is interested in children and how to improve their health and development.

In years to come, we hope that the children in the study will be proudly telling friends and relations that they are one of the Children of the 90s and in response to the query on how did that start, they can hand them this book to read.

Jean Golding
Director: Children of the 90s

1
Tackling the Impossible

'Finding out more about pregnancy and childhood health has got to be a good thing' - Michele Pilgrim: first mother to enrol for the Children of the 90s survey.

'If they didn't do things like this they'd never know anything' - Samantha Coombs: 10,000th mother to enrol for the Children of the 90s survey.

'I find it exciting to be part of it, and see the results coming through, knowing that a little bit I've done has helped them on their way' - Shona Lambert: mother with Children of the 90s.

Michele, Samantha and Shona are just three of the 15,000 West Country mothers who are taking part in the Children of the 90s survey into pregnancy and childhood. It's a survey which will be providing new information about why some children grow up healthy and others don't, and suggesting directions for further research, well into the next century. It's huge in its scope, unique in the material it has assembled.

Michele and her fellow mothers are convinced that children for decades to come will be happier and healthier because of the hours they've spent hunched over 52-page questionnaires - trying to work out how many days in the past month they've drunk 'more than two pints of beer, four glasses of wine or four pub measures of spirit': or to decide who usually wins any battles of will with their toddler ('me', 'my toddler', 'about even', 'neither of us').

Back in the late 80s, when Doctor Jean Golding, now Professor of Paediatric and Perinatal Epidemiology in the Institute of Child Health at Bristol University, and the survey's Director, was putting together the first proposals, there were many professionals who thought she was biting off more than she could chew. True, there'd been similar surveys before, getting parents to fill in questionnaires. And they'd been successful. But if this one was to provide the sort of information Jean and fellow researchers needed, it would have to be on a scale not attempted before. It would have to make unprecedented demands on health workers and parents. Surely, there were just too many obstacles?

'Mothers are too busy to help with something this big.'

'Morning' sickness. Backache. Exhaustion. And then the sleepless

EXPECTING A BABY?

Do you know about Children of the Nineties — an exciting study of children starting in pregnancy?

For further information please fill in a card or Telephone: Bristol 256260

Dr. Jean Golding
Children of the Nineties
Institute of Child Health
24 Tyndall Avenue
Bristol, BS8 1BR

How it all began.

nights. The nappies. The regurgitated meals. The teething. And of course, exhaustion.

Haven't pregnant women – let alone mothers with new babies – got enough problems? How many women in their right minds would take on any further tasks?

15,000 turned out to be the answer in Avon, where Children of the 90s was launched in September 1990. Over 80%, in fact, of the women in the area whose babies were due to be born between April 1991 and December 1992. Mothers from 14 years old to 47. University lecturers and mothers who could barely write; chartered accountants, mushroom pickers, butchers, and hairdressers; women from the affluent heights of Clifton, the bed and breakfast accommodation round Temple Meads and the neat estates of Nailsea; from isolated country hamlets and crowded council estates; single mothers and those into their third marriage; mothers pregnant with 'test-tube' babies and those whose pregnancies were completely unplanned.

Of those who originally signed up, only 10% have dropped out, and women who have left the area have stayed deeply involved – completed questionnaires are currently arriving at the survey office in Bristol from Sri Lanka, the Gambia, Pakistan, Nigeria, Cambodia, Canada and Australia. Even the 1,000 or so mothers who have miscarried, or whose babies have died, have helped the survey further by filling in special questionnaires.

By their child's first birthday, each mother has answered something like 3,000 questions, 5,000 by its second. They've provided samples of urine, hair, blood and finger nails – and hair and nails from their babies and partners as well. They've even generously donated their placenta and a slice of umbilical cord to the survey's unique biological archive!

Many of them have helped make regular measurements of radiation and pollution in and around their homes, and a thousand have trekked across Bristol every six months for additional Children in Focus clinics – *not* too much fun with a four-month-old and possibly a disgruntled toddler in tow!

'The government felt it would never work,' comments Jean Golding. 'After all, look what we're asking people to do – by the time these babies are two, their families will have received and sent back 17 questionnaires.' But, busy though the average mum may be, Children of the 90s has proved that she is prepared to *make* the time for something which she thinks may benefit the children of the 2000s.

'You can't expect midwives to help. They're far too busy.'

Keen mums out there. Keen professionals back at the Children of the 90s office. How to get them together?

Mothers completing questionnaires.

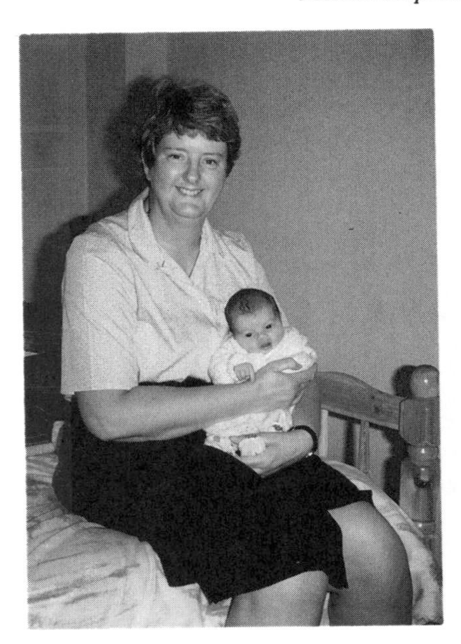

Faith Owen, community midwife, with Children of the 90s baby, Naomi Williams.

One thousandth Child in Focus, Ross, with his mother Sue Collins.

The Post Room.

Keying in the results.

Newspapers, obviously, and cards in surgeries and libraries - survey staff used every form of publicity they could think of to recruit mothers to the survey. At one point the Bristol *Evening Post* never seemed to be without a Children of the 90s article.

But if the survey was to recruit most of the area's mothers early in their pregnancy, it had to have help from their midwives. They were already stretched to their limits: it seemed unreasonable to expect them to put much effort into encouraging women to enrol in a survey which would actually make yet more work for them.

But, remembers Pam Holmes, who liaised with local maternity hospitals for the survey, once midwives had become convinced that the survey could work, 'they couldn't do enough to help.' The study's team of interviewers were at every scan clinic in the area during this time - 16 per week. 'We tried to see every expectant mother as they waited to have the first picture taken of their baby. Many had joined Children of the 90s already, but it was an ideal time to encourage more and thank those who had.' Between them, the midwives and interviewers helped recruit 85% of the mothers who signed up.

Their help didn't stop there. They went to endless trouble to collect blood and urine samples during pregnancy, and, even as they coped with the dozens of tasks immediately following each birth - cleaning up, paperwork, and caring for mother and baby - they made time to process placentas and cord slices for the biological sample store.

'How reliable are mothers anyway?'

Most mothers, after all, aren't medically trained. They get things wrong. . . They're harassed, they don't get enough sleep, they have too many responsibilities. They fill in questionnaires with one hand while they spoon creamed carrot into dribbling mouths with the other. Can research workers really base a major study on the observations of exhausted amateurs?

In 1989, Children of the 90s ran a pilot survey to see just how reliable mothers were. A small sample were asked questions about previous births, whether there had been any complications, what medicines or treatment they had had.

Their answers were then compared with their medical notes. Over 95 per cent of their answers tallied with what was recorded there, proving very clearly that mothers' observations are accurate and their memories trustworthy.

'You'll never get the funding.'

No doubt about it: *this* is the real problem, the one which at times has come very close to crippling the whole study.

OUR MOTHERS AROUND THE WORLD

Number of mothers in each country

Australia 8
Belgium 5
Brazil 1
Cambodia 1
Canada 3
Cyprus 1
Denmark 1
France 10
Gambia 1
Germany 13
Holland 5
Hong Kong 1
India 3
Ireland 3
Italy 1
New Zealand 1
Nigeria 1
Poland 3
Portugal 2
Puerto Rico 1
Saudi Arabia 1
Senegal 1
South Africa 2
Spain 2
Sri Lanka 1
Switzerland 1
Turkey 1
Uganda 1
United Arab Emirates 4
USA 13
Zimbabwe

'Good thing we're using recycled paper. There wouldn't be any rainforests left otherwise.'

Children of the 90s currently costs about £1 million a year to run. Not a lot when you remember what that covers: salaries for 70 or so full and part time staff, printing and posting the questionnaires and, of course, buying and maintaining the computers on which everything depends. Two callers to the BBC phone-in programme 'Voices of the West', who themselves had lost a baby and brought up a severely disabled child, described the cost as 'a drop in the ocean, very, very little' and 'a bargain. . . a few pennies'.

But chasing £1 million each year takes up most of Jean Golding's working life. Where does she manage to get it from?

So far, about a third of the costs have come from government bodies like the Department of Health and the Ministry of Agriculture, Fisheries and Food. Up to 20% has come from charitable organisations such as the National Asthma Campaign or the Anne Diamond Cot Death Appeal. Sponsorship from commercial companies has covered a further 20% of the costs, and most of the remainder has come from the United States, where researchers already see this as a survey of international importance.

There's also been what might be called 'support in kind'. Bristol University has let the survey use university premises rent-free. Avon hospitals have lent space in their freezers to store biological samples. Probably the most unusual 'gift' has been 12,000 placentas, generously 'donated' back to the survey by the pharmaceutical company which, until recently, bought them from Bristol's maternity hospitals.

It's been a hand-to-mouth existence, but Children of the 90s has stayed solvent - just!

Go into the survey's cramped offices, and you know immediately that people here care about what they're doing. Early in the morning, late into the evening, even at weekends, there's likely to be someone there at work. It may be one of the survey's gallant army of retired volunteer telephone-answerers, a research statistician or a programmer snatching some extra time on the computer. Lunch breaks are almost unknown. Despite the low wages, the lack of job security - most staff have only the shortest of short-term contracts - there's a sense of excitement, of people working on something they know is important.

Mothers feel the same way. 'I hope your research is successful in every way,' scribbled one on the back of her first questionnaire. 'Thank you for letting me do my part.'

2

A Survey is Born

Whatever's happening to our children's health?

Child health experts today know surprisingly little about what makes and keeps a child healthy.

We all know that - in the rich countries of the West at least - far fewer children die young now than a century ago. Back in 1900 roughly one child in three died before it reached its fifth birthday. Today the figure is down to one in a hundred.

But how *healthy* are the children of the 1990s? Infectious diseases like measles, tuberculosis and whooping cough have largely disappeared, thanks to nation-wide immunisation programmes. Better food and living conditions have done away with many of the old childhood scourges like rickets. But some childhood illnesses are actually increasing.

At Bristol's Southmead Hospital, for example, admissions of children with asthma have doubled in the past ten years. Nationally there are twice as many 10-year-olds with diabetes as there were twenty years ago. Many more children are suffering from eczema.

Even the link between poverty and sickness is more complicated than it once seemed. It's there all right - the children of poorer parents are still less likely to survive than those of richer parents - but other factors are emerging as important. Children in centrally heated double-glazed homes, for example, actually seem *more* likely to have respiratory problems than those in poorer housing.

The experts confer!

It was facts like these that led the World Health Organisation in 1985 to assemble a group of child health experts from all over Europe at a week-long meeting in Moscow. The meeting's brief was to recommend ways for European governments to improve the health of children in their countries by the year 2000.

That week the experts discovered how little they actually knew.

'Eventually it was clear we did agree on some things,' remembers Jean Golding, Britain's only representative at the meeting. 'We agreed that we didn't know clearly what the problems were concerning illness and disability in children in Europe. We didn't know whether the problems in one country were similar to those in another. And, even where we did

Death rates over time

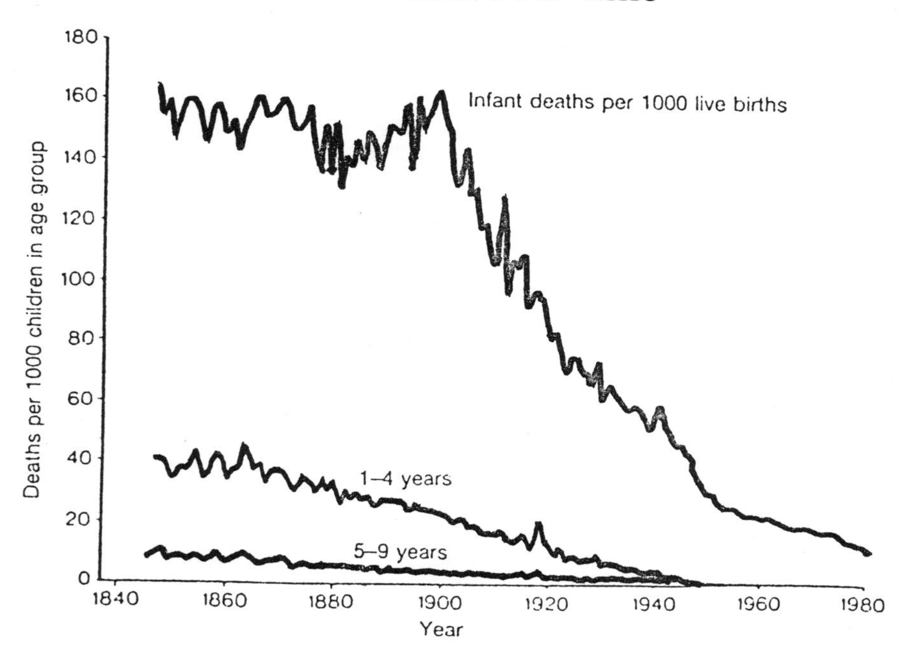

know what the problems were, we had no idea how to prevent them.'

'We realised it was crucial,' she says, 'to get a clearer idea of what diseases were affecting children in the different countries of Europe. And at the same time we needed to identify which features in the environment might be causing these diseases.'

There was, the experts agreed, only one way to find the answers to these questions: by going to the people with inside knowledge – the mothers and fathers of the children of Europe – and asking them what was happening to their children.

Another survey?

Were you born in the week of 4–11 April, 1970? If you were, the chances are that from time to time you still get asked to fill in lengthy questionnaires about your health or attend clinics to see how you are getting on.

Three nation-wide child health surveys, launched in 1946, 1958 and 1970, have taught us much of what we now accept as gospel about child development. The advantages of breast-feeding, the harmful effects of smoking in pregnancy and the link between poverty and ill health were

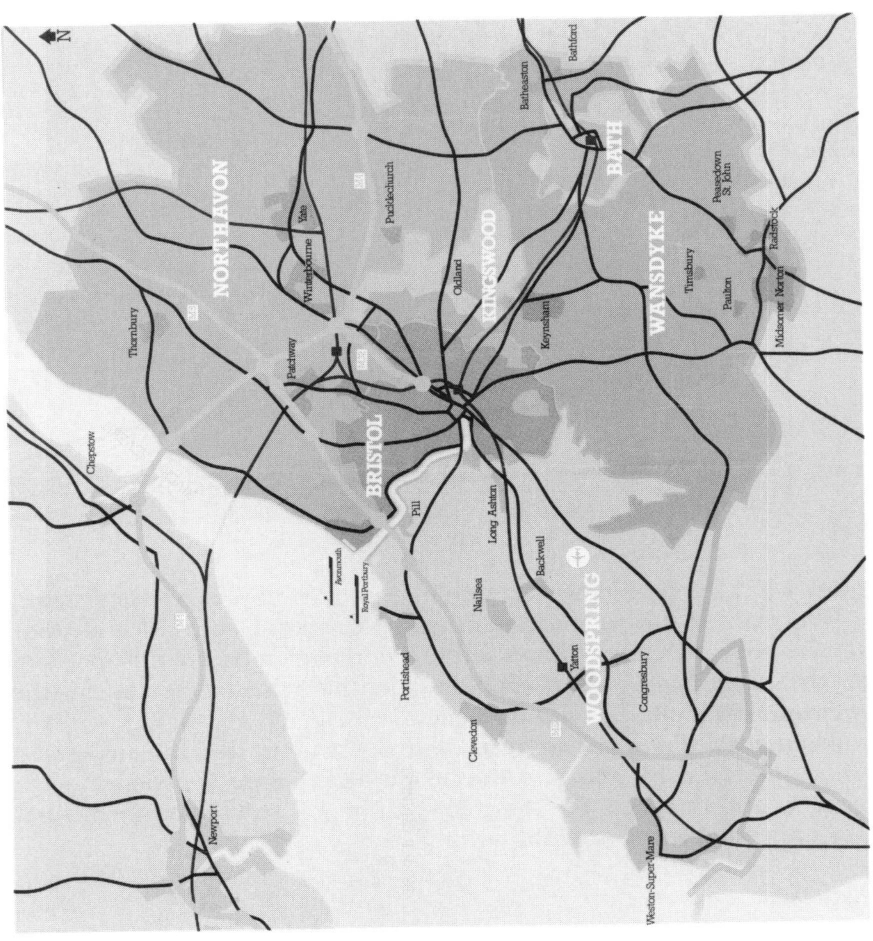

Avon county – mothers living in Woodspring, Bristol, Kingswood, Northavon and part of Wansdyke were invited to take part.

all discovered or confirmed by following the progress of children covered in these surveys.

But, having learnt so much already, why launch yet another survey twenty years on?

Well, partly because those twenty years have seen huge changes in the environment that children are growing up in. The chemicals they are exposed to have increased and changed - there are more cars on the roads, their parents are using different cleaners in the house. Social habits have changed - more mothers are out of the house doing paid work, more families are eating pre-cooked frozen meals. Some of the changes will probably have been beneficial, some harmful, and some both or neither, but the experts are unsure which have been which.

And partly because the earlier surveys, though they have revealed so much, were what Jean Golding describes as 'blunt tools'. Because Children of the 90s is following children born over a longer period (21 months rather than a week) and from a narrower geographical area, its findings will be more reliable and more precise. Seasonal variations - those winter colds! - will be taken on board, and the people interpreting the results will know what sort of environment babies living in BS13 or BS11 are growing up in.

Why Avon?

'When you think about it,' explains Jean, 'Avon is the ideal place for a study like this. It's very defined geographically, and people don't move out. In Oxford, for example, where I used to live, ten per cent of the city's young families moved out of the city each year. In Bristol it's more like two per cent, and people tend to be very cooperative. It has a very similar composition of rich and poor, tall and short, fat and thin, bright and dull, young and old, urban and rural to that of the UK overall.'

And the rest of Europe?

One of the traditions at World Health Organisation meetings is that someone with a good grasp of English is always made the meeting's 'rapporteur', the secretary who writes up the notes on each day's proceedings, and reports back the next day. 'This means,' says Jean, 'that, while the rest of the group are able to relax in the evening and go out for a meal or visit the theatre, the rapporteur is stuck in the hotel writing up her report.'

She may have missed out on a few Moscow restaurant meals, but through her role as rapporteur at the 1984 meeting Jean was to emerge as central co-ordinator of the European Longitudinal Survey on

Jean Golding and Thalia Dragonas from Greece.

Designing the study

Rimma Ignatyeva from Russia.

Dennis Henshaw at Chernobyl.

ELSPAC Centres

1. Avon, UK
2. Isle of Man
3. Yaroslavl, Russian Federation
4. Brno, Czech Republic
5. Znojmo, Czech Republic
6. Bratislava, Slovakia
7. Athens, Greece
8. Ivano-Frankiwsk, Ukraine

9,10. Kiev right & left banks of the River Dnipro

11. Dniprodzerzhynsk, Ukraine
12. Mariupol, Ukraine
13. Krasnyj Louch, Ukraine

<u>Countries planning and piloting:</u>

14. Malmö, Sweden
15. Tartu, Estonia
16. Varajdin, Croatia
17. Mallorca, Spain - no longer participating.

Yaroslavl, Russia: one of ELSPAC's study centres.

Questionnaire check-in, Ivano-Frankiwsk, Ukraine.

Pregnancy and Childhood, or ELSPAC as it's known in the trade. Seven separate countries as far apart as Greece and Russia are already running their own surveys, using their own versions of the Children of the 90s questionnaires. Others are keen to join – when they can get the money.

Some of the European surveys face huge difficulties – they've even had a problem finding paper in the Ukraine. But health workers at many of the survey centres are desperately keen to find out, and let the world know, what is happening to their children: part of the Ukrainian study is being run in an area where most of the mothers are evacuees from Chernobyl. This is the first opportunity health statisticians in some East European countries have had to work with 'uncooked' figures, and they're eager to start collaborating with scientists from the West.

All in all, Children of the 90s and its partners in Europe are likely to transform our understanding over the next few years. In ten years time we should know far more about how children grow up in modern industrial societies.

No wonder the Americans are interested!

3

Doing it Right

'Tread softly because you tread on my dreams'

Pregnancy, childbirth and caring for a young baby are emotional experiences for most parents, even when everything is going fine. Joy, exhaustion, worry and elation pile on top of each other, until the strongest, most competent people can find themselves with their normal emotional defences in ruins. For the single teenage mother or the couple whose relationship is weakening, parenthood can bring huge stress and confusion. Parents who lose their baby or learn that it is handicapped may have to cope with agonising grief.

Respect for parents, and a concern not to cause them any pain during a possibly vulnerable period of their lives, govern the Children of the 90s approach. These concerns are reflected in the firm, considered ethical guidelines which control the survey.

Like all medical research projects, Children of the 90s had to have its structure and methods approved by the Ethics Committees of its local health authorities. In addition, because a survey of this size and complexity is constantly throwing up ethical issues, it has its own ethics committee, whose members include doctors, lawyers and (originally) a theologian. They meet regularly, and their job is to make sure that the survey follows the guidelines originally agreed with the health authority committees, and that it continues to treat parents with respect and sensitivity.

Protecting parents

One of the committee's jobs is to judge the contents of each new questionnaire, and see if the proposed questions are likely to cause stress or distress to parents answering them.

Most parents seem prepared to face difficult truths when they fill in their questionnaires. Many bravely give answers which almost certainly cause them pain. Some comment at the end of a questionnaire that writing such answers has actually been helpful to them. This was particularly true of mothers filling in the special questionnaires about their miscarriages.

But obviously no one wants to subject parents to unnecessary suffering – or to have them drop out of the survey as a result – and it's the ethics committee's job to keep an eye open for questions that probe too deeply.

Possibly the most controversial questions in the whole survey are the ones asking parents if they have suffered any form of sexual abuse as a child. Though they are specially reminded of their right not to answer these or any other questions, it's clear that just reading them has been painful or embarrassing for some people. Many who answered have expressed anxiety at what they've written - for some, it's the first time they've ever revealed their childhood experiences.

Parents showing this degree of courage obviously need to be assured that their answers really are confidential, and are likely to help other parents and children.

Keeping it confidential

Children of the 90s staff have two main tasks - linking things up and keeping them separate. They can press a button and link almost any set of records with almost any other set - that's what the whole survey depends on, after all. But they also have to make it absolutely impossible for anyone else to link parents' names and addresses with the answers they have given in their questionnaires.

The survey's security systems are complex, depending on a series of passwords known only by the computer staff, and changed regularly. The research staff don't know them: even the Director is kept in ignorance. Researchers needing extra information from a particular set of mothers - ones who are breast-feeding, for example, or who suffer from asthma - are given the names and addresses of mothers who answer that description, mixed in with an equal number who don't. When they follow up those mothers, they will have no idea who is in which set.

The whole system seems to be fool-proof. But the technological problems are the easy ones to solve.

What's harder is the dilemma faced by some other survey staff. What should they do if they read a questionnaire from a mother who is clearly at risk of harming herself or her baby? Many mothers have help from survey interviewers to fill in their questionnaires: what should the interviewers do if they come across a baby - or a mother - with bruises or a black eye?

Parents have been promised confidentiality and that promise must be honoured. But clearly no responsible adult can turn a blind eye to someone in danger, least of all a baby. So a compromise has been worked out: staff who are seriously worried about a mother or baby that they have seen have a hot-line to senior members of the ethics committee, who will decide whether to alert the mother's GP or health visitor, unscrambling the computer's systems if necessary. No action is ever taken over anything on the questionnaires unless the mother signs her name.

Respecting parents

One mother's informed, responsible choice is another mother's eccentric

Linda with her Child of the 90s, Dwayne.

The project's nerve centre.

lunacy. Children of the 90s parents run their lives in all sorts of different ways, and the survey has to be open, and avoid making assumptions or too many judgements.

As the questionnaires are compiled, there are many heated discussions. How can they take full account of the diets and customs of Asian, Jewish or black parents? How can they be worded to cover fathers who are looking after their babies full-time, or mothers whose partner is another woman?

Staff know that every time they word a question so that a parent feels excluded, they risk losing his or her co-operation. They wouldn't claim always to have got it right, but they hope that parents will sense that the key-note of the whole survey is respect for the job they are doing and the choices they make.

4

The Cardboard Boxes Come and Go

Time marches on

And the Children of the 90s are growing and changing with each passing month.

Visit the survey office at most times of the year, and you'll see one result of that growth - box upon box upon neatly labelled cardboard box, piled on shelves, in corridors, even at times in the cloakrooms. All full of completed anonymous questionnaires, waiting to be keyed into the computer.

June each year is the most crowded time on the cardboard-box-front. Come July, the survey takes on 30 or so maths and psychology students, referred by their tutors, who spend the summer working through the boxes accumulated over the past year. Checking each questionnaire for unclear or contradictory responses, they agree on appropriate coding, and type out any written answers - all those 'other' or 'please describe' lines that come after the tick boxes. In the summer of 1994 they processed 45,000 questionnaires, ready for passing on to the bureau which actually types them into the computer.

Finally, with their answers safely stored in the computer, the keyed-in questionnaires move to their resting place: 800 feet of shelving, and a steadily increasing proportion of the floor, in a university basement. 'We're looking for more space,' observes Hugh Simmons, the survey manager, pensively.

Back in the Children of the 90s office, Mary Evans and her team in the survey post-room deal with over 800 completed questionnaires each week. In the early days, when a steady stream of questionnaires was needed to record the progress of each pregnancy and then the many rapid changes that children go through in their first months, the Post Office van was collecting up to five sacks of questionnaires a day for distribution to parents. With the children now settled down into toddlerhood, Mary is still sending out nearly 1,000 questionnaires a week.

The questionnaires are the real heart of the survey: 14,000 sets of minutely detailed information about the situations in which the children of the 90s are growing up, and the ways in which they are

The questionnaires come in by the thousand.

. . . and keep on coming!

developing, physically, intellectually and emotionally. It's all there: diets, social structures, home and work environments, parental attitudes, and medical histories for two generations back.

It may be another generation before we discover the full significance of some of that information, but already a quick browse through the questionnaires throws up all sorts of interesting facts.

- 93% of all mothers, for example, have taken the contraceptive pill at some point in their lives: on average they started using it at the age of 16 or 17. 70% of the mothers were deliberately trying to get pregnant; 2% had been trying for three or more years. Half-way through their pregnancy over 5% of the mothers had thought of harming themselves during the previous week. Most mothers felt that they had been in control during their labour and well supported by the medical staff.

- Boys seem more prone than girls to just about every illness except rashes, and their mothers give them medicine more often. More girls than boys sleep in their parents' rooms at the age of six months. And they stay cooler: more boys' bedrooms are heated through the night; 44% of boy babies sleep with a duvet but only 29% of the girls.

- At the age of six months, one child in five has ten or more books of their own; another one in five has none.

All the facts emerging are interesting: what they mean for the babies' development will only become clear as they are matched with the other information being gathered in the survey.

Smoking grandmothers

This was the item that really hit the headlines in 1994.

It's already well known that mothers who smoke during pregnancy are more likely to have stillbirths or babies who weigh less than they should. Their babies are more likely to suffer cot deaths.

Smoking mothers in the survey have also turned out to have a whole range of other problems during their pregnancy. They were admitted to hospital more often than non-smoking mothers, and far more of them said they often felt unwell during their pregnancy. They had more problems with vomiting, urinary tract infections and thrush.

Non-smoking mothers with a smoker in the house or a smoky atmosphere at work were also more likely to have problems. Women who were passive smokers took longer on average to get pregnant, and were more likely to suffer from headaches and be admitted to hospital during their pregnancy.

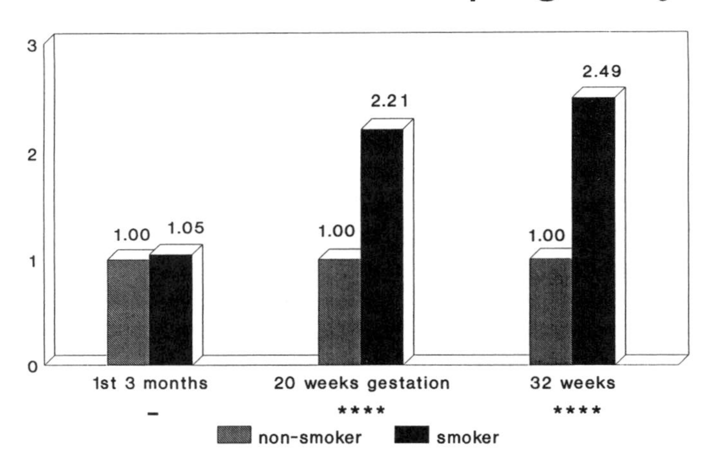

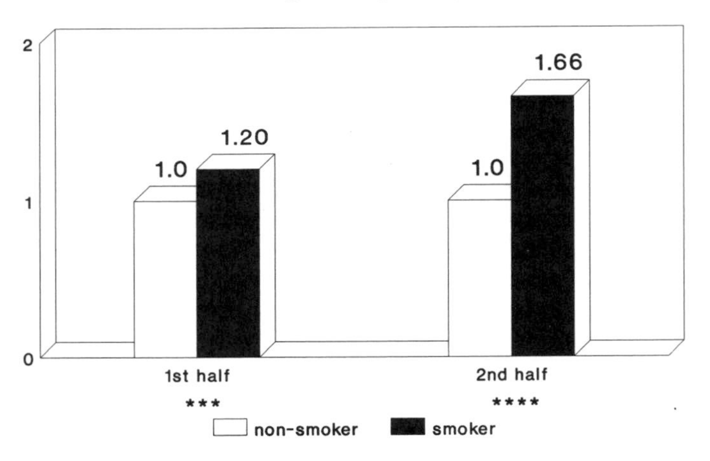

But it was the findings about the 'smoking grandmas' that really caught media attention when they were announced. Children of the 90s mothers, it appeared, whose own mothers had smoked during pregnancy were more likely to have had problems with bleeding in their own pregnancy, and to have miscarried.

More research is needed, but it's beginning to look as though a mother who smokes during her pregnancy is affecting the long-term sexual development of her unborn children, and so is probably already affecting her unconceived grandchildren.

Out for a breath of fresh air.

Back or front?

In one respect the survey's timing was perfect. In November 1991, just about half-way through the year when the Children of the 90s were being born, the government launched its 'Back to Sleep' campaign. Statistical research in New Zealand had shown a clear link between putting children to sleep on their fronts - as advised for decades by health professionals - and cot deaths. The UK campaign advised mothers to start putting their babies down on their backs, and also to make sure the babies' bedrooms weren't too warm.

The Children of the 90s graphs show that most mothers started following this advice immediately. Common practice changed almost overnight, and the survey was there to record the effect of these changes.

They have turned out to be quite startling. Babies placed on their backs were less likely to wake at night, to choke during feeding, to suffer from wind, to visit their GP, to have been given antibiotics or cough medicines. By the time they were six months old, those placed on their fronts were more likely to have had earache, coughs and runny noses. They were less likely to be listening to people, turning their heads towards sound, more likely to have been referred to the hearing assessment centre.

One of the aims of the Children of the 90s survey had been to see if other, unexpected, problems had increased with the sudden changes in the sleeping habits of the nation's under-ones. Quite the reverse, it would seem: the only problems that seem to increase when a child is laid to sleep on its back are nappy rash and cradle cap.

Following the 'before' and 'after' babies over the coming years may give us more information and provide all sorts of clues for future research.

'Mystery over shock figures'

So proclaimed the *Bristol Observer* in September 1993, reporting one of Children of the 90s' most unexpected findings: the 'bleeding by postcodes' mystery.

Sixteen per cent of mothers in the study reported that they had had an episode of vaginal bleeding in the first three months of their pregnancy. But the sixteen per cent don't live randomly scattered across Avon, as might be expected. Nor do they live clustered in just one particular part of the region - which, of course, could be an exciting clue to environmental causes.

They seem to live concentrated in particular postcode districts, but not necessarily in neighbouring ones. So a band including areas like Portishead, Clifton and Hartcliffe (which actually vary considerably from each other) has a very low incidence of bleeding. Right next to this band are areas like Westbury-on-Trym and Bedminster, where there is a very high incidence.

The findings don't mean that pregnant mothers in Westbury or Bedminster are at particular risk - bleeding may be alarming to the mother, but it's not related to miscarriage. The bleeding considered here was among mothers who did not miscarry. What it does mean is that Children of the 90s has come up with a finding that is currently leaving doctors, statisticians and environmental scientists completely baffled.

Good news for mothers of twins

You may have felt ill, but you were probably just as happy during your pregnancy as those with lighter burdens.

Researchers looking at the mental health of mothers expecting twins were surprised to find that their levels of stress and depression were no higher than those of other pregnant women. Though they were physically ill more often, emotionally they were in much the same shape as anyone else at the ante-natal clinic.

Food for thought here: researchers think this is probably because they *expect* to experience a high level of physical discomfort and inconvenience, and are therefore less dismayed by it, than many other mothers. In addition, they arouse more interest and sympathy among others, and this helps them to feel cared for and supported. Could it be that, with more realistic advance information and more social support, other mothers would actually have fewer emotional problems during pregnancy?

Medicines

The thalidomide tragedy in the 60s showed that drugs which heal or soothe a mother can have a devastating effect on her unborn child. Most pregnant mothers who have to take any medication usually find themselves wondering if it's having any effect on their baby.

Children of the 90s researchers looked to see what drugs mothers most commonly took during their pregnancy. The answers have been surprising. 'We had all assumed that pregnant women took the thalidomide tragedy to heart and avoided medication as much as possible, but far from it', said Neil Hawkins, the researcher involved. It was much more unusual for a mother *not* to take medication than the reverse. Most medicines and pills taken were bought from the chemist and so their doctors knew little about this.

How safe are drugs like aspirin and paracetomol? Do they endanger the child in any way? Many of the drugs used have never been tested for safety in the pregnant mother. Might they result in changes in the behaviour of the child, make him or her more susceptible to infection or likely to develop asthma? Children of the 90s will be able to answer these questions as the children get older.

'Everyday' drugs

And so to the drugs most of us happily gulp down every day: the cups of tea and coffee, the glasses of cola.

All contain caffeine, a drug which, we already know, passes easily through the placenta to the unborn child, as well as being quickly absorbed into breast-milk. Many mothers find they are simply unable to stomach tea or coffee during pregnancy: the taste nauseates them. Is the mother's body defending the unborn baby from substances which may harm it? Do mothers who reject such drugs in pregnancy have healthier babies?

As to alcohol, mothers who drink very heavily are more likely to have babies with serious developmental problems, but what about the occasional glass of wine or beer? Early evidence from the study indicates that moderate or occasional drinking results in a slightly healthier baby than avoiding alcohol altogether.

Most of these tentative findings need more research before we can be sure that the links really exist, let alone be convinced that, for example, putting a child to sleep on its back actually 'causes' cradle cap. But they are exciting glimpses of the knowledge that Children of the 90s could be unlocking over the next ten, twenty, thirty years.

5
Putting Men in the Picture

It was fairly late in the planning of the study that the research team realised that a major figure was missing. They had not thought about actually asking the father (or the mother's partner) how things were for *him*. There were plenty of questions in the questionnaires asking the mother how she thought her partner felt, but the idea of asking him directly was a new one.

As soon as the researchers realised this, it seemed extraordinary that no other similar survey should have bothered either. There have been a few studies of fathers, but based only on interviews with individuals. Nobody knew even whether fathers would be prepared to fill in questionnaires and return them. Would fathers be happy to take part in a study that was focused on the child? There were no other studies to learn from, or to help work out what were appropriate questions to ask fathers.

Hastily the survey asked a recent father, Daniel Illsley, to suggest the sort of questions that he felt fathers ought to be asked. A number of other fathers and mothers, as well as experts in the field of parenting and family life, were also asked. The result is a set of questions that are unique in their depth and breadth.

In order to assess just how well they work, the questions were tried out in Greece and Britain, and a comparison of the results showed that fathers in both countries were able to fill in the questionnaires and did so willingly.

The key question was how to ask partners to take part. For a start, there was no way of knowing their names. Clearly, contact could only be made through the mothers. So every mother was asked if she would like her partner, if she had one, to take part in the survey. She was sent a questionnaire and an explanatory letter to pass on to her partner.

There is no way of knowing how many mothers have actually invited their partners to take part. What survey staff do know is that every time questionnaires are sent to mothers to hand to their partners, between 60% and 70% come back completed. It's not as high a return as the mothers' 85%–90%, but it is an extremely valuable set of information.

For the first time ever, we have a clear picture of how fathers feel about the pregnancies of their partners. In the middle of the pregnancy, one third of the fathers said they were overjoyed, half were pleased, and only 9% had mixed feelings or were unhappy about it. Interestingly,

Daniel Illsley writing a questionnaire.

although two-thirds of the fathers didn't mind whether the baby was a boy or a girl, more of those who did have a preference wanted a boy. This contrasted dramatically with the mothers, more of whom wanted a girl.

The fathers were less likely than the mothers to be vegetarian (3.5% were vegetarian or vegan compared with 5.5% of the mothers), and almost equal numbers of fathers and mothers had been smokers at some time (53% of fathers). In all, 6% of the fathers had smoked cannabis in the six months before the pregnancy, and almost all were regular consumers of alcohol. Only 4% stated that they did not drink at all. In fact, they were certainly not goodie-goodies: 21% had been in trouble with the police before the age of 17, 10% had been expelled or suspended from school, and 12% had truanted regularly.

Possibly as a result of these chequered pasts, 17% had no qualifications at all, but 19% had a university degree. 11% were unemployed.

The fathers completed a further questionnaire when the child was eight weeks old. Most had actually been present at the birth – 15% of them under pressure! – and for 80% it had been a wonderful experience. They were less enthusiastic about the sleepless nights – a third felt they were still not getting enough sleep. Possibly as a result, over half reported feeling irritable, and 12% felt weepy or tearful at times.

What about the 'New Man' we hear so much of? Difficult to judge how many Fathers of the 90s qualify! Around half reckoned they helped 'a lot' with shopping or washing up, but it was downhill after that, with a third helping with the cooking, a quarter with cleaning and a mere 12% with washing clothes.

It was a different picture when it came to involvement with their new babies, however. Nearly all of them played with the baby at least once every two days, and a magnificent 70% changed the baby's nappy regularly. Over half put the baby to bed at least as often as the mother did, and between a quarter and a half helped with feeding (even at night), bathing, or taking him or her out for walks.

The picture that has emerged is of fathers very much involved with the birth and first months of their child's life. Children of the 90s will be sending a questionnaire each year to the fathers, to see how this involvement continues, and how it affects the child's development.

This chapter has talked mainly of 'fathers', but actually it's been up to the mother to decide who, if anyone, her 'partner' is. In most cases, it's the father of her child, whether or not she is married to him. In some cases, it's another man; in a number of cases it's a woman. Children of the 90s staff have tried to throw away any pre-conceived ideas as to what is 'right' or 'normal', and study what is actually happening.

Situations change, too. Partners have changed from one year to the next. Some, tragically, have died. Some who seemed to be devoted fathers have left home. Fathers have been left looking after the child when the mother has died or left home - are they now 'partners' or 'mothers'?

Such rapid change is a fact of life in the nineties. What we do not know is what effect it has on children. Do they develop better if their parents stay together in unhappy relationships or if they split up? How do they react to step-parents, step-brothers and step-sisters? Several partners commented on these aspects in their questionnaires: 'hope this research with families will be of help to others,' was one anonymous comment; 'pity more work is not done in society to help families.'

The willingness of 'partners' to fill in questionnaires ('is there a special place allotted in hell for those who make up questionnaires, or for those who answer them?' wondered one weary dad) will give us a far clearer idea of how families are actually functioning in the nineties.

6
The Stuff of Life

A Monday morning in March 1993. The phone rings in the Children of the 90s office. A worried man at the other end: it appears that the rather antiquated freezers at Bristol University Veterinary School have finally packed up. With it being the weekend, the fault has only just been detected. Which means that temperatures in the freezers are now up to -11 degrees Centigrade. And rising slowly. . .

It's a little known fact that frozen urine needs to be kept at a steady -20 degrees Centigrade. And stacked in the dying freezer were 28,000 Children of the 90s frozen urine samples. (Fortunately, the 50,000 blood samples were elsewhere.)

Over the next few days temperatures rose inexorably, as Jon Pollock, the survey's deputy director, rang all round Avon, trying to find a new, cold, home for the precious samples. Local supermarkets were sympathetic, deeply appreciative of the splendid work being carried out by the survey - but curiously unwilling to make room among the fish fingers in their own freezers. Other university and hospital freezers were full.

Nobody seemed to be buying it.

In the end, Jon solved the problem by hiring a commercial trailer freezer, to hold the samples until purpose-built freezers could be installed in one of the Bristol University basements.

'She said something about 8,000 roasting placentas?'

Then there was the day of the arson attack. Another phone call to the Children of the 90s office, this time to announce that fire had broken out at the removals warehouse which was providing temporary storage space to 8,000 Children of the 90s placentas from babies born at Southmead Hospital.

Survey staff dashed off through the Bristol traffic, only to find that police had cordoned off the area round the warehouse. Hours of suspense followed. Had the placentas gone up in flames? How would they announce this tragedy to the survey mothers? Finally they were allowed in to inspect the damage. The outer containers were slightly smoke-blackened – but inside the placentas, preserved in formalin, were untouched. Today they, too, are safely stored with placentas from other hospitals, in yet another hospital basement.

Nowhere else in the world is there anything to match the huge bank of biological samples – hair, nails, urine, blood, cords and placentas – collected by Children of the 90s. Each sample is identified with a number which enables it to be linked with the relevant questionnaires, and each sample has its own story to tell.

Black boxes in white buckets

The placentas, for example, explains Jem Berry, Bristol University's Professor of Pathology, are like 'black box flight recorders', storing information about possible inherited conditions and about the baby's progress through the pregnancy. They reveal whether the baby suffered at any stage from a shortage of oxygen, or whether his or her mother smoked during the pregnancy, and a host of other facts.

When this 'record' is analysed and linked to the written record contained in the questionnaires, we will have a far clearer idea of how events in pregnancy affect the baby's subsequent development. Already we suspect that a tendency to heart disease, strokes and diabetes is present before birth: studying the Children of the 90s placentas may confirm that, and also indicate what causes that tendency.

As he escorts the visitor along the rows of white plastic buckets, each containing ten neatly labelled plastic-wrapped placentas, Jem reels off the statistics: 12,500 placentas – six tons in all – preserved in 40,000 litres of formalin. With memories of the warehouse fire firmly in the past, this really is a resource which will be telling us more for decades to come about life before birth.

Decoding the evidence

It'll be a while, however, before we really start tapping the information coded into these lumps of tissue, because it takes time just to examine and test each one.

The same is true of the other samples. Just cutting the frozen umbilical cords into smaller lengths, ready for different tests, has taken four medical students the best part of two long summer vacations. The same is true of the blood and urine samples – getting on for 60,000 samples have had to be thawed, measured out into smaller containers, and refrozen to await analysis.

It's fiddling and tiresome work – ask any of the students! – but the range of information stored in the samples is immense. The mother's blood will show what pollutants, especially lead and other 'heavy' metals, she's been exposed to. These pollutants can also be measured in the umbilical cord, so we'll get a better idea of what gets passed from the mother's blood into the baby's system. We'll be able to see what the effect is on the baby's long term development.

Nail clippings and hair from both the child and its parents will also show what new pollutants – including mercury – the child is exposed to as he or she grows up. For the first time, we'll have reliable evidence about the effects of pollution on our children.

There are all sorts of other links to be made between the mother's

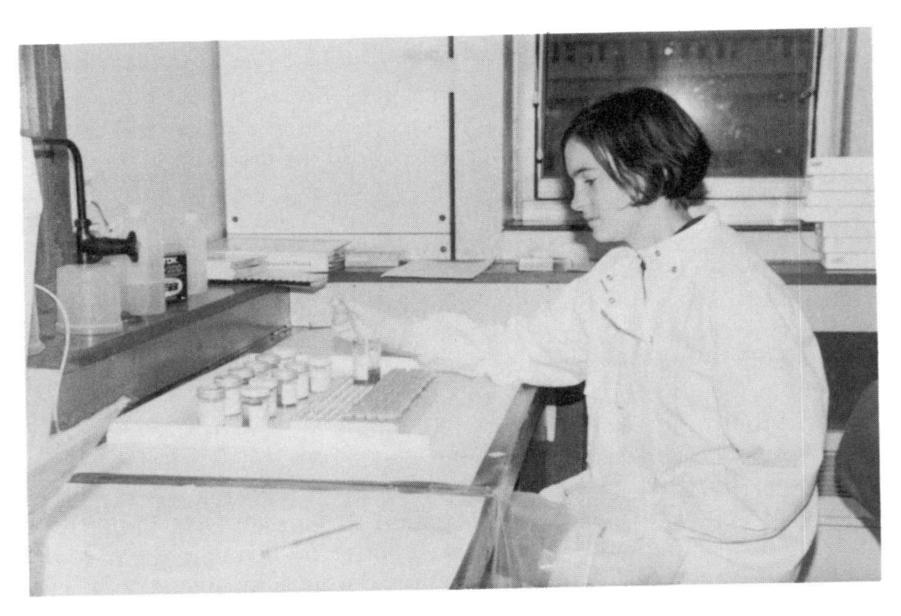

Some of the 60,000 blood and urine samples.

blood and the baby's cord or cord blood: hormone levels, allergic reactions, levels of drugs like aspirin, tranquillisers or nicotine. The result should be an increasingly clear and accurate understanding of how the mother's actions and environment affect her baby.

Pregnant women make choices every day of their pregnancy which may or may not affect their unborn baby. The expectant mums of the 2000s will have a good deal more proven knowledge to base their decisions on.

7
An English Mum's Home is Her Castle

But how healthy an environment is it nowadays for her and her children?

The air we breathe

Caroline Brown was one of the 150 Children of the 90s mothers who agreed to measure levels of air pollution in and around their homes.

'It was really complicated,' she told the BBC programme 'Voices of the West'. 'The people organising the air pollution survey - some laboratory somewhere - explained to us that it would mean that we would have three tubes to put out every month and it wouldn't be as simple as just pushing them all out at the same time and taking them all in at the same time.

'One of the tubes, I think, had to go out for two or three days and the other one had to go out for a week, and the other one had to go out for a month - it was something like that - different lengths of time for different colour-coded tubes. And you had to put them in your bedroom and some of them had to go outside. And you had to mark your calendar, get them in and write the times that you put them out and took them in, and you had to try and get it as close as possible.

'So anyway I said yes I'd be prepared to do it, but obviously I had to ask Richard and he said yes he'd do it and it's a jolly good job he did because he's the one that used to remember to take the tubes down. I used to fill everything in, but he was the one who said "oh don't forget you've got to do the tubes at seven o'clock tonight" or whatever. He was wonderful because he was the one that kept me organised.

'I suppose there were times when we felt "oh God" - because you get reminded when the new tubes would come through the door - but I never once thought "oh I can't be bothered to do it". I just thought "I don't know whether I'll be able to fit it in" and I thought "well I've got to because it's part of the study" and I feel it's a real privilege to take part - you really feel like you're doing something that's going to make a difference.'

Caroline has a particular reason for being keen to take part in the survey. She's been conscious of 'the environment' ever since the age of 17, when she started to work on oil tankers. 'By the time I was 21,' she remembers, 'I was perfectly convinced that carrying vast quantities of hydrocarbons from one continent to another just so that they could get burnt to produce yet more pollution in another continent was not necessarily the best way of doing things.'

But her general interest in the environment has become a very personal concern in recent years. 'I live in Hartcliffe,' she explains, 'and we've got a factory which regularly pumps out vast quantities of horrible-smelling stuff, and I'd always been against them putting this factory here. I'd even questioned quite closely the Chair of the Planning Committee at the time when it came here – I felt it was really inappropriate to put such a factory in a great big estate. However, it's here and I thought 'well at least if the study shows something there they might take some notice of it.'

As adults we breathe in enough air each day to fill an Olympic-sized swimming pool. A small baby breathes in a similar amount relative to its size – into lungs that are barely equipped to cope with the complex mixture of gasses and chemicals that now surround us.

It's vital that we learn what that mixture actually is, and what it's doing to our babies' bodies and brains. Measuring the air in public areas isn't really enough – we need to know how much external pollution seeps into the home where babies spend most of their time, and how much additional pollution is produced in the home: what else do those air 'fresheners' do to the air?

The basic information which Caroline and other mothers are providing about the air quality in and around their homes is valuable in itself. When this information is linked with information from their Children of the 90s questionnaires, we will begin to know whether, for example, the factory Caroline so hates is just a smelly nuisance – or a real threat to her child's development.

The data's all there – when will we start getting this information? Not just yet – this part of Children of the 90s had run out of money, but more funding has just appeared and information will be processed as soon as possible.

A similar study, which may shed light on a possible cause of problems for premature babies, has been funded by British Gas. 1,200 mothers, including 200 with babies born prematurely, took part in this fortnight-long test. A less demanding task this time, compared with all Caroline's tube-popping – they simply left one measuring tube in their child's room and placed one outdoors to measure nitrogen dioxide levels, and filled in an extra questionnaire about the heating and cooking facilities in their homes. But it was an extra chore for a busy mother – particularly one coping with the extra demands of a prematurely born baby – and Children of the 90s staff were delighted with the 91% response rate.

Some like it hot – or do they?

Not so long ago most babies slept in bedrooms where a crisp winter night would send temperatures zooming down below freezing. Today – at least for the 90% of homes with central heating or storage heaters – those exquisite frosty patterns on the inside of the window pane are a thing of the past.

Then a whole range of childhood illnesses was blamed on the cold. Today there's a strong suspicion that over-warm homes may be almost as harmful to health, and that cot deaths in particular may be caused by hot bedrooms.

The Cot Death Research Trust, along with HTV and the South West Electricity Board, has funded studies with 8,000 parents to see how high they are keeping temperatures in their babies' bedrooms, and what effects this is having on their babies' health. Half the selected parents were sent a nursery thermometer and asked to fill in regular room temperature charts.

Charts were still coming back in the spring of 1994 – so watch this space to find out if you ought to consider turning the thermostat down a degree or two!

The ground beneath us

The South West is well known for the high levels of radon – naturally occurring radioactivity – in its soil. What effect does this have on the health of the people living there? One suspicion is that there's a link between radon and miscarriages, and Children of the 90s has obviously been well placed to test this theory.

'Marvellous news, Mrs Jones. You know we got a tumble dryer last week? Well, now we've got a RADON DETECTOR!'

Mothers – including 250 who had recently lost their babies during pregnancy – were keen to help by recording radon levels in their living rooms for a couple of months. In fact, several mothers who were about to move house when invited to join the study asked to be put on a waiting list to join later.

Fortunately, a willing benefactor was around to match their willingness. A grant of £10,000 is covering the cost of analysing the radon detectors, and checking whether radon levels are higher in the homes of the mothers who miscarried.

Homes for healthy babies

And finally, the Children of the 90s questionnaires themselves – what are they telling us about the best surroundings for a baby to grow up in?

Commonsense tells us that poor housing must equal poor health, but researchers have found it's not that simple. Some surveys, for example, have 'shown' that children living in more overcrowded homes are more likely to have accidents: others have 'shown' they aren't. Even researchers who have found real links between housing and health problems usually find that there are other possible explanations for the problems.

Children of the 90s is producing the most detailed picture we've yet seen of the relationship between health and housing. Few areas of Britain have a wider range of housing than Bristol and its surrounding towns and villages. And the Children of the 90s questionnaires are finding out just about everything that can be found out. Does your roof leak? Do you have the space to sit and eat in your kitchen? Have you wallpapered your bedroom in the last year?

The picture emerging is quite reassuring. Nine out of ten mothers are 'satisfied' or 'fairly satisfied' with their home. More than half see their neighbourhood as friendly, clean and pleasant.

But what of the one in ten who aren't satisfied with their housing, the half who are less enthusiastic about their neighbourhood? Parents' answers are beginning to show a real link between housing and health.

Mothers living in rented accommodation, especially in council housing, are more likely to have health problems and be depressed. If they use mains gas-fires they're more likely to have coughs; those who use coal fires are much less likely to have migraines.

For babies there seems to be a similar pattern. The poorer their housing – and the more dissatisfied their mothers are with it – the more likely they are to have had high temperatures, blood in their stools or vomiting attacks.

Most people in Britain fight a running battle in their homes against the twin enemies of damp and mould. Not surprisingly, nearly half the

Proportion of mothers who were depressed

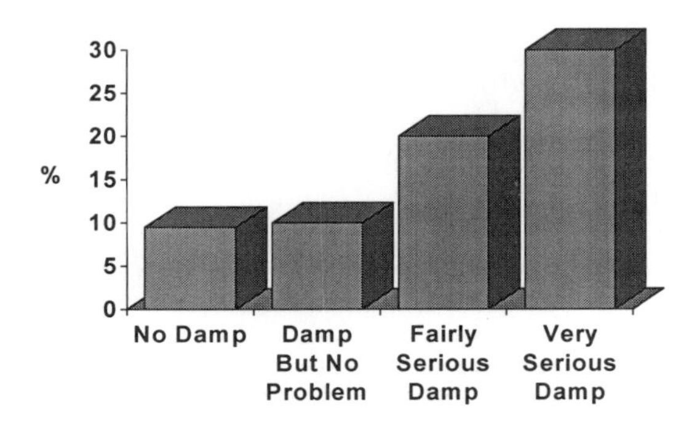

Wheezing attacks

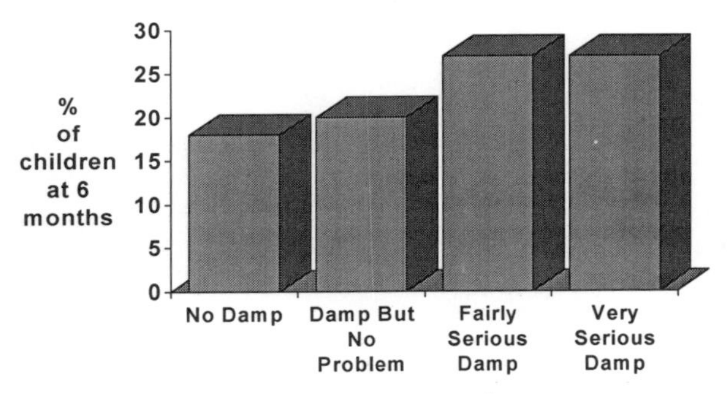

Emergency home visit by GP

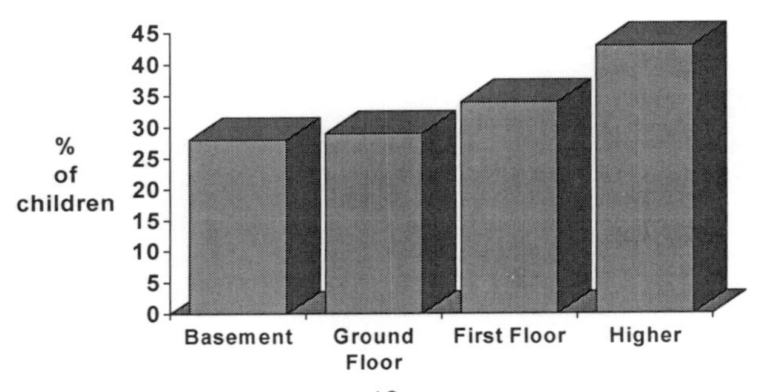

Children of the 90s mothers report problems with one or both. And the more serious they consider their problem to be, the more likely their babies are to have needed emergency visits from their GPs, to have had wheezing attacks, high temperatures, colic or accidents.

Children of the 90s researchers have barely begun to examine all these links between housing conditions and health. The links don't necessarily mean that poor housing conditions *cause* the health problems they're linked to. There are all sorts of other possible causes, and the researchers need to examine them as well.

But, for the first time ever, the information is there, keyed into the computer from mothers' questionnaires. The statisticians are now arriving. . .

8
Children in Focus

Depth to match the breadth

Children of the 90s is giving us possibly the broadest understanding we've ever had of a region's babies and their development. Children in Focus adds the depth to the picture.

By the time their children are two years old, most Children of the 90s mothers will have answered something like 5,000 separate questions. But spare a thought for the lucky mothers in the survey whose babies were born between June and December 1992, who were invited to join the additional Children in Focus study. The foolhardy ones who agreed to take part have brought their children to Children in Focus clinics in Bristol every 4–6 months, to be weighed, measured and put through various standard tests, all to provide more detailed information than the questionnaires can give.

Making it fun

'It's amazing that they keep coming,' says Sue Sadler, the Clinic Manager. 'There's nothing in it for them. The children are not ill, and they get no treatment. The only benefit to the child is that their vision is screened and defects followed up, and their parent is told if the child's haemoglobin is below a certain limit. Otherwise parents make this huge effort purely for the health of future generations.'

And it *is* an effort. Just lugging a small Children in Focus child across the centre of Bristol, possibly with an older sibling – or, increasingly, a younger one – in tow, can write off the rest of the day for many mothers. And then there are the ones who've moved, but are still coming back specially for the clinics from Sheffield or Cornwall . . .

Because the children have been so meticulously documented throughout their lives, they are, says Sue, 'a rare and valuable resource'. And they have to be treated as such, to make sure they and their parents enjoy their visits enough to want to come back again and again.

So help is provided with transport. Petrol costs and fares are paid, and a parking space reserved for them behind the old Homoeopathic Hospital, where the clinics are held. Taxis are provided for parents without transport – with drivers specially trained to give a harassed mother the help and tolerance she may need! Once arrived at the clinic, many a mother *must* have to repress a sigh of pleasure as siblings are

'Amazing, they keep coming,' says Sue Sadler.

whisked away to be entertained by the receptionist. There are even extra receptionists taken on in the school holidays to cope with older sisters or brothers.

For the children, the clinic is a riot of bright posters, plants and mobiles, with a regularly changed selection of toys, as well as welcoming staff who become more like family friends with each visit. The children are offered a small present at the end of each clinic - a toothbrush, a book, a height chart: anything that might appeal to the child who's feeling just that little bit frazzled and over-tested. (Donations welcomed from sympathetic manufacturers or suppliers!)

The parting present is the bit that appeals particularly to two-year-old Emma Webster-Green, according to her mother Joanna. She likes to sit and 'read' her book: 'Children Nineties. Children Nineties. Children Nineties. Like story, Mum?' She enjoys the clinics, and likes to chat about them afterwards to her father, her sister Becki and foster-sister Kishana. 'She loves watching the little soldier measuring the gunk in her ears,' says Joanna. 'She talks a lot about the little man, and now she even has an imaginary one of her own! He lives in my jeans pocket apparently, and, whenever she feels miserable, she grabs him out of my pocket, stands him on her hand and gives him lots of kisses. It does get people looking at us in supermarkets!'

Making it work

Administratively, it's a nightmare. Even computers can splutter when asked to draw up staff and parent rotas for 1,200–1,400 children to go through four different tests or procedures in an hour every six months. And in the children's first year it was every four months: they were starting on the clinics for eight month olds before they'd finished testing the four month olds. '"No overlap," I begged Jean Golding,' remembers Sue. 'Commonsense said it just couldn't be done with the staff and accommodation we had available. But there was no real alternative. So we did it, and we made it work. The triumph of hope over experience.'

For the staff, the clinics are where the whole Children of the 90s survey comes alive, as they meet the children and parents who are otherwise known to them only as ticks in the boxes of anonymous questionnaires.

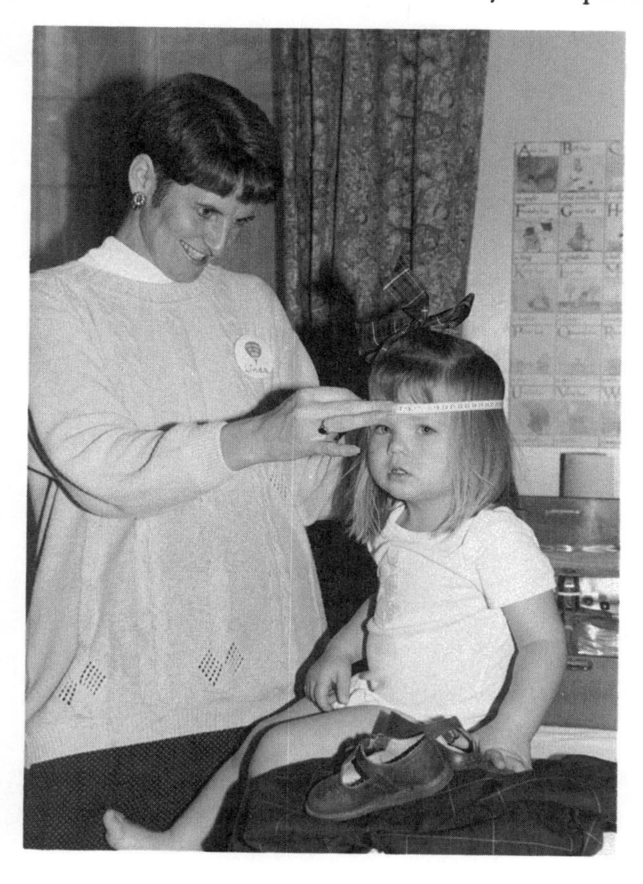

Looking at . . .

. . . *ears.*

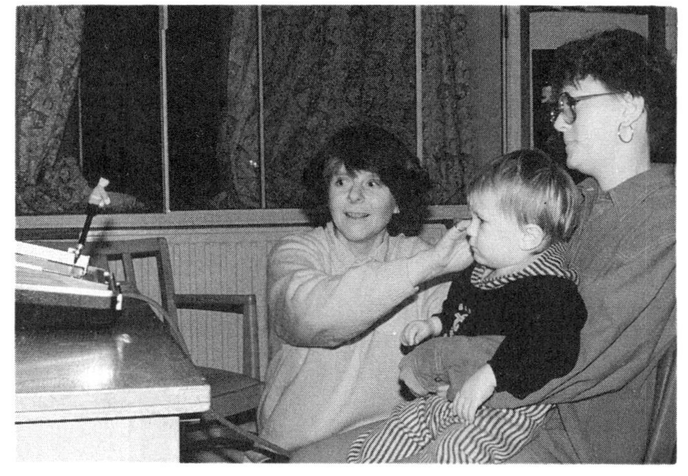

. . . *speech.*

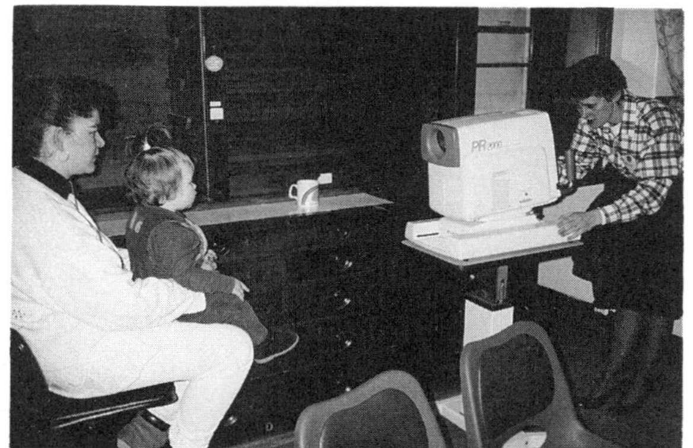

. . . *eyes.*

Particularly exciting are the first clinics for each new age group, when staff who have become completely attuned, for example, to the world vision of eighteen month olds have suddenly to adapt to the vastly more sophisticated attitudes and vocabulary of two year olds. 'We all have to adjust fast,' remarks Sue. 'All the things we thought were safe suddenly aren't any more. We have to rush around putting new catches on doors, and moving breakable objects or essential papers six inches higher.'

The first findings

Like most Children of the 90s data, the information researchers are collecting from the Children in Focus clinics will be teaching us more about child development for decades to come. The older the children grow, and the more the researchers are able to link together information from the clinics and other findings from the questionnaires, the clearer our understanding will become.

But the Children in Focus researchers already have many questions they are confidently expecting to find answers to. Areas they are particularly interested in include diet, growth patterns, incidence of anaemia and the causes and effects of hearing and sight problems. Are reduced-fat foods good or bad for growing children? Do children whose mothers have difficulties getting to a food shop eat as much fresh fruit as other children? And does it matter?

Does 'glue ear' lead to speech problems? Do pre-school sight tests have long-term benefits? Is it true that children's fingerprints indicate which are most likely to have high blood pressure and heart disease? If it is true, what early pregnancy experiences are linked with particular fingerprint patterns in the child?

How does the way parents interact with their child affect its development? How do their own childhood experiences affect the way they look after their children? Are there any differences between children looked after full-time by their own parents, and those looked after during the day by someone else?

Findings are already beginning to emerge: new ideas about how very small children concentrate on new objects, about the effects of a vegetarian diet during pregnancy, about identifying anaemia in young babies, about children who may be particularly likely to develop asthma and eczema.

Not surprisingly, some of the findings have been unexpected, and following them up will be one of the great challenges for the survey in the coming years. To quote Sue: 'we don't yet know what it all means, but we're going to follow it up and find out.'

9
The End in Sight?

Meeting the children

'Now that our oldest children are three,' wrote Sue Sadler in a 1994 newsletter for doctors and health visitors, 'and show no signs of having a six-month break from growing older (something we have long considered would be a Good Thing) we are having to face a new challenge. How best to organise full developmental, intellectual, and health checks of all 14,000 children when they are seven years old.'

The Grand Finale to the survey, in both Avon and the other European centres, comes in 1998, when survey staff will come face to face at last with the survey children - all 14,000 of them.

The plan is for every child to have a physical examination, similar to those formerly carried out by school nurses. They will be weighed and measured, and have their blood pressure, sight and hearing tested. Survey staff will be looking at the skills they've developed and their progress at school.

Little details like how and where to carry out the tests are still being worked on! Visiting schools with a team of staff might have seemed a good idea - but there are currently 321 state primary schools in the Children of the 90s catchment area, all with seven-year-olds spread between their junior and infant parts. Possibly clinics like the Children in Focus ones will be the best way of organising the examinations, but it will mean running at least two clinics a day six days a week.

But these are mere details, minor problems, compared with the ones the survey has already faced and solved . . .

Hearing from their mothers

Children become daily more complicated beings, as they master new skills, adapt to new situations, and learn to think their own thoughts.

Over the next few years the questionnaires will be reflecting these changes. 'Much of it, I'm afraid,' says Hugh Simmons, 'will be more of the same.' But the questionnaires will also be following the children as their speech develops, as they learn to draw, paint, make works of art from two toilet rolls and a handful of macaroni, read and write, and solve life's great problems like how to get the left shoe on the left foot.

There will be questions on their growing interests, how they get on with children and adults outside their family, how they react to creche,

Children in Focus clinic.

playgroup, nursery school and, finally, Big School itself. Their diet may well change over the years, especially when they start school: this may affect their development in ways which we know little about.

And the questionnaires will also be building up a picture of how they react to new baby brothers and sisters, to bereavement and loss, moving home, their parents' changes of job or unemployment. How do their parents react to these events? And how do parents set about guiding their children through each new stage in the often exciting, often painful, business of growing up?

'We are here to help,' Pam Holmes says. 'The team are very aware of how much we ask of our mothers. Seven years is a long time to be filling in questionnaires, especially at a time in life when there are very few moments to sit and think. Small children are very time-consuming. We make many home visits to help a mum through a questionnaire. All she needs to do is ask, by phoning the number on every questionnaire.

'Personal contact between the team of interviewers and the mothers also finds out why someone hasn't sent back a questionnaire: "I never received it"; "the dog ate it"; "I was in hospital having baby number 3." We would love to speak to everyone personally, and tell them how valuable they are to the survey. Each and every one contributes to its continuing success.'

What else is coming?

Or: the Thwarting of the Tooth Fairy . . .

Hair and nails are such a valuable record of how the body is affected by its environment that the survey is hoping to continue collecting samples from the children each year until 1998.

Round about 1996, of course, the children will be providing new biological samples, as their first milk teeth drop out. Parents will be asked to throw aside all moral scruples, and shamefully betray their child's trust by removing one tooth from beneath the pillow *before* the Tooth Fairy gets there and sending it to Children of the 90s.

We have assurances from the Survey Manager that all teeth will eventually, after analysis, be left on a velvet cushion under a large toadstool in a moonlit forest glade, for collection by the proper authorities . . .

Talking of teeth . . .

Dentists are keen to know more about the effects on the unborn child of amalgam fillings during the mother's pregnancy. After all, this is the time when most mothers make a special point of visiting the dentist, and when they are particularly likely to need fillings.

Children in Focus mothers have been asked to authorise their dentists to show their dental records to survey staff. If the dentist is willing to co-operate, staff will be recording all the amalgam fillings given to each mother, both in the months before conception and during her pregnancy. They will be able to match this with information about her child's development.

'I think I'd rather go into labour.'

Funds for the future

'When we started planning this study,' remembers Jean Golding, 'we had this fond idea that once the government heard about the importance of the survey our financial problems would be non-existent, that they would see this as a good investment. In actual fact, nothing of the sort happened, and we were told that we would have to raise money by going for specific little projects and putting them all together and trying to make the whole amount that we needed.

'So I spend most of my time chasing money from all sorts of places, from the United States, charitable trusts like the National Asthma Campaign and a number of other sources like private companies. Although it's hard work it raises our awareness of the many questions we will be able to answer.'

Funding – or the lack of it – was a major problem in the first years of Children of the 90s. But, almost certainly, the survey has come safely through its most critical period. Survey workers and the parents of Avon have proved that it *is* possible to run a survey this large and complex. Possible funders are seeing it as an exciting and valuable way to use their money. And, even if the survey had to close tomorrow, the information they have collected would be eagerly pounced on by other researchers the world over.

A final word . . .

. . . has to be from the mothers who, with their partners, have made it all possible.

Let's go back to 1991, when the first cardboard boxes were just filling with the first questionnaires, and nobody could be *quite* sure that the whole thing really would take off. The comments scribbled anonymously on the backs of many early questionnaires express the enthusiasm which mothers have brought to the double task of bringing up their baby and filling in their questionnaires:

'Cannot complete as I have just started labour. Wish me luck!'

'We've enjoyed the questionnaires. They've been very thought-provoking, and given us an insight into what we are doing and where we are going. Let's all continue with our good work!'

'One hour after I completed this questionnaire, baby has just smiled for the first time!'

Looking to the future.

10

Children of the 90s

The Families at a Glance

A FEW FACTS AND FIGURES

• **During pregnancy . . .**

Of the mothers

89% had the use of a car. 88% had the use of a phone.

72% were living in mortgaged homes.

47% were living in homes with some damp, mould or condensation.

93% had used the contraceptive pill.

29% had been blood donors.

51% had never smoked, 20% were smoking more than one cigarette a day; most smokers started when they were between 10 and 16 years old.

25% usually drank more than 1 glass of wine at the weekend.

60% had been on a diet at some time.

65% felt that becoming a mother had given them new interests.

71% felt they had become more irritable during pregnancy.

8% were in management positions, compared with 17% of their partners.

About 60% liked their job and had friendly supportive colleagues.

20% had had a miscarriage.

13% had had an abortion.

70% had been deliberately trying to get pregnant; 2% had been trying for three or more years.

Of their partners

59% had no confidence that the state would support them through trouble; 67% felt their families would help them through financial difficulties if they could.

25% had no religious faith. 53% described themselves as Church of

England, 7% as Roman Catholic. 10% went to a place of worship at least once a month.

Nearly 80% were overjoyed or pleased when they learnt that their partner was pregnant. Nearly 90% wanted to be with her through her labour.

13% had played truant from school after the age of 11.

• After the birth . . .

79% of mothers loved their baby immediately they were born. 15% took up to a week to do so.

• At four weeks . . .

28% of babies had a lot of wind all the time.

54% of babies were being at least partly breast-fed.

77% of babies were looking at their mother's face when being fed. 65% were following her with their eyes. 34% often smiled and 11% often laughed.

• At six months . . .

Only 16% of babies were sleeping through the night. 17% woke more than once every night – some as often as 8 times.

23% of all parents always gave their child a cuddle when he or she woke. 28% never did.

• At eighteen months . . .

12% of toddlers had had chicken pox.

55% of mothers had a battle of wills with their toddler at least once a week. 49% of these reckoned they won most often, and 22% that it was about even.

45% of mothers sometimes gave their children fruit to stop them crying. 17% gave them sweets.

12% of toddlers often refused to eat a meal.

82% of partners cuddled their toddler nearly every day.

74% of babies could build a tower of 3 bricks, and nearly all could pick up a small object like a raisin. 54% were already helping with simple tasks in the home.